JUL 0 5 2006

W9-CQF-372

RHINOCEROS

WILDLIFE IN DANGER

Louise Martin

Rourke Publishing LLC
Vero Beach, Florida 32964

www.rourkepublishing.com

PHOTO CREDITS:
Cover photo © Tom/Pat Leeson

EDITORIAL SERVICES:
Pamela Schroeder

Library of Congress Cataloging-in-Publication Data

Martin, Louise, 1955–
   Rhinoceros / Louise Martin.
      p. cm. — (Wildlife in danger)
   ISBN 1-58952-021-1
   1. Rhinoceroses—Juvenile literature. 2. Endangered species—Juvenile literature.
    [I. Rhinoceroses. 2. Endangered species.] I. Title

QL737.U63 M378 2001
599.66'8—dc21

                                     00-067074

Printed in the USA

TABLE OF CONTENTS

RHINOCEROSES

Rhinoceroses are one of the best known animals in large zoos. But in the wild, rhinoceroses have become highly **endangered**.

Endangered animals are in danger of becoming **extinct**. Extinct **species**, or kinds, of animals have disappeared from the Earth.

White rhinos, the largest of five species, are sometimes called square-lipped rhinos

Rhinoceroses are huge, plant-eating **mammals**. The only land mammals bigger than rhinos are elephants and large hippopotamuses.

There are five species of rhinos, the Sumatran, Javan, greater one-horned, black, and white. The largest rhinos, the whites, weigh up to 8,000 pounds (3,600 kilograms). But being big hasn't helped rhinos survive. In fact, the rhinos' size has made them easy targets for hunters.

Just 50 to 60 Javan rhinos remain in the wild

WHERE RHINOS LIVE

The remaining 2,400 greater one-horned rhinos live in the borderlands of northeast India, Bhutan, and Nepal. The last 60 Javan rhinos live only on the Ujung Peninsula of Indochina and in the Cat Loc Nature Reserve of Vietnam.

Oxpeckers pick insects from the back of a black rhinoceros in an African swamp

The 300 Sumatran rhinos live in parts of Malaysia, Sumatra, and Borneo. The 2,700 black rhinos live in 10 African countries, including Kenya, Zimbabwe, and South Africa. Southern white rhinos live in much of southern Africa. The last 30 northern white rhinos live only in Congo's Garamba National Park.

Rhinos live in **habitats**, or homes, where they can find favorite foods and nearby water. African rhinos generally live in grassland or open forest habitats. Asian rhinos live in a variety of habitats, from grasslands to wetlands and mountain forests.

Rhinoceros horn is made of keratin

A black rhinoceros with its twin horns

RHINO HORNS

African and the shaggy Sumatran rhinos have two horns on their heads. Greater one-horned and Javan rhinos have one. A rhino horn is made of **keratin**, the same material of which fingernails are made. Like a bar of soap, rhino horn can be shaved with a knife.

Rhino horns have much to do with why their owners are endangered.

Greater one-horned and Javan rhinos have just one horn

RHINOS IN DANGER

Rhino horn is very valuable to certain groups of people in Asia and the Middle East. For centuries, many Asians have believed that rhino horn is powerful medicine or magic. It isn't, but facts don't always change old beliefs.

In 1991 rhino horn was selling for as much as $23,000 per pound ($50,000 per kilogram). **Poachers** were willing to take great risks to kill rhinos and sell their horns.

These white rhinos live at the San Diego Wild Animal Park in California

A big buyer of rhino horn was the little Middle Eastern country of Yemen. Men in Yemen wanted carved rhino horns for the handles of their knives. Between 1970 and 1984, about half of all rhino horns went to Yemen.

By 1987, Yemen had mostly stopped rhino **imports**. But the demand for rhino horn as medicine continued. And it continues to this day, especially in Taiwan and China. Loss of habitat is also a problem for rhinos.

African rhinos usually live in open, busy country

SAVING RHINOS

Rhinos are protected by laws wherever they live. Several countries have made strong efforts to stand behind their laws. Nepal, for example, protects 460 greater one-horned rhinos with 1,000 soldiers in Chitwan National Park. India has 1,200 greater one-horned rhinos in Kaziranga National Park. The park had just 300 rhinos in the 1960s. South African countries have brought the southern white rhino back from almost sure extinction.

Poachers kill rhinos to remove their horns and sell them for medicine and ornaments